L♥VE

YOUR

LIFE

© Copyright 2021 - All rights reserved.

You may not reproduce, duplicate or send the contents of this book without direct written permission from the author. You cannot hereby despite any circumstance blame the publisher or hold him or her to legal responsibility for any reparation, compensations, or monetary forfeiture owing to the information included herein, either in a direct or an indirect way.

Legal Notice: This book has copyright protection. You can use the book for personal purpose. You should not sell, use, alter, distribute, quote, take excerpts or paraphrase in part or whole the material contained in this book without obtaining the permission of the author first.

Disclaimer Notice: You must take note that the information in this document is for casual reading and entertainment purposes only. We have made every attempt to provide accurate, up to date and reliable information. We do not express or imply guarantees of any kind. The persons who read admit that the writer is not occupied in giving legal, financial, medical or other advice. We put this book content by sourcing various places.

Please consult a licensed professional before you try any techniques shown in this book. By going through this document, the book lover comes to an agreement that under no situation is the author accountable for any forfeiture, direct or indirect, which they may incur because of the use of material contained in this document, including, but not limited to, —errors, omissions, or inaccuracies.

CRISTIE JAMESLAKE

MY DAILY REVELATION

MY DAILY REVELATION

"Nothing can dim
the light that shines
from within."

MY DAILY REVELATION

MY DAILY REVELATION

"If you have good thoughts they will shine out of your face like sunbeams and you will always look lovely."

MY DAILY REVELATION

MY DAILY REVELATION

"Am I good enough?
Yes I am"

MY DAILY REVELATION

MY DAILY REVELATION

"Who you are inside is what helps you make and do everything in life."

MY DAILY REVELATION

MY DAILY REVELATION

"Good riddance to decisions that don't support self-care, self-value, and self-worth."

MY DAILY REVELATION

MY DAILY REVELATION

"I'm giving you permission to root for yourself and while you're at it root for those around you, too."

MY DAILY REVELATION

MY DAILY REVELATION

"We do not need magic to transform our world. We carry all the power we need inside ourselves already."

MY DAILY REVELATION

MY DAILY REVELATION

"I have never ever focused on the negative of things. I always look at the positive."

MY DAILY REVELATION

MY DAILY REVELATION

"We must accept finite disappointment, but never lose infinite hope."

MY DAILY REVELATION

MY DAILY REVELATION

"I am deliberate and afraid of nothing."

MY DAILY REVELATION

MY DAILY REVELATION

"Your perspective is unique. It's important and it counts."

MY DAILY REVELATION

MY DAILY REVELATION

"Your life is already a miracle of chance waiting for you to shape its destiny."

MY DAILY REVELATION

MY DAILY REVELATION

"If you really think small, your world will be small. If you think big, your world will be big."

MY DAILY REVELATION

MY DAILY REVELATION

"Embrace the glorious mess that you are."

MY DAILY REVELATION

MY DAILY REVELATION

"Gratitude is a celebration we are all invited to."

MY DAILY REVELATION

MY DAILY REVELATION

"The ultimate truth of who you are is not I am this or I am that, but I Am."

MY DAILY REVELATION

MY DAILY REVELATION

"We must be willing to let go of the life we planned so as to have the life that is waiting for us."

MY DAILY REVELATION

MY DAILY REVELATION

"Your life is about to be incredible."

MY DAILY REVELATION

MY DAILY REVELATION

"I'm better than I used to be.
Better than I was yesterday.
But hopefully not as good as
I'll be tomorrow."

MY DAILY REVELATION

Put yourself first!

"Nothing is impossible. The word itself says 'I'm possible!',"

www.ingramcontent.com/pod-product-compliance
Lightning Source LLC
LaVergne TN
LVHW061625070526
838199LV00070B/6581